You Need to Know People

Fr. Mark Ngwah

Published by Mark Ngwah, 2024.

While every precaution has been taken in the preparation of this book, the publisher assumes no responsibility for errors or omissions, or for damages resulting from the use of the information contained herein.

YOU NEED TO KNOW PEOPLE

First edition. August 28, 2024.

ISBN: 979-8227120847

Written by Fr. Mark Ngwah.

"Once you master reading people nobody can ever play with you."

Toast Quote

"We are like books. Most people only see the cover, the minority read only the introduction, many people believe the critics. Few will know our contents"

"You Need to Know People":

Do you yearn for deeper connections and a more meaningful life? In this insightful exploration of human behavior, you'll embark on a journey of self-discovery alongside the author. Through keen observation and a thirst for genuine connection, you'll gain a fresh perspective on the people who surround you.

This work delves into the power of nonverbal communication, the importance of honesty and authenticity in relationships, and the art of navigating complex social dynamics. With an emphasis on understanding the intricacies of human nature, this book reveals that everyone you meet is like a gift, wrapped uniquely with their own experiences and qualities.

You'll discover:

- How to read people with greater clarity and understanding, by observing their body language, tone, and even the silence between their words.
- The importance of setting healthy boundaries while remaining open to the lessons each person brings into your life.
- Strategies for fostering meaningful connections and recognizing the value of each individual, regardless of their outward appearance or behavior.
- The transformative power of letting go of negativity and embracing the diverse array of human experiences.
- How to prioritize experiences and genuine connection over fleeting possessions, finding joy in celebrating life and its many relationships.

Filled with relatable anecdotes and thought-provoking quotes, this book is a valuable resource for anyone seeking to:

- Improve their communication skills by becoming more

attuned to both spoken and unspoken cues.
- Build stronger, more fulfilling relationships by seeing each person as a mirror and a bridge on the path to personal growth.
- Cultivate a more positive and compassionate outlook on life by understanding that every person you encounter is a part of your journey.

Whether you're a seasoned observer of human behavior or simply seeking to understand yourself and others better, **"You Need to Know People"** offers a roadmap to a more fulfilling and connected life. It encourages readers to embrace the adventure that is humanity, recognizing that people are astonishing, and that every interaction holds the potential for transformation and growth.

Preface:

Be curious. Read widely. Try new things. What people call intelligence just boils down to curiosity.

Educate yourself. When a question about certain topic pops up, google it. Watch movies and documentaries. When something sparks your interest, read about it, Read, read, read, study, learn, stimulate your brains. Don't just rely on the school system, educate that beautiful mind of yours.

About the Author

Fr. Mark Ndifor OFM Cap is a devoted Catholic priest affiliated with the Franciscan Capuchin Friars, where he has faithfully served his community for over two decades. His journey into priesthood has been marked by a profound commitment to compassion, empathy, and the spiritual well-being of others.

Fr. Mark's academic background is rooted in the study of human psychology, holding a Master of Arts degree in Counseling Psychology and a Bachelor of Arts in Counseling Studies from the University of Manchester. He further honed his expertise with a Higher Diploma in Counseling Studies and is a respected member of the Kenya Association of Professional Counselors, upholding rigorous standards of professional conduct in his practice.

His scholarly pursuits have delved into significant societal issues, particularly exploring the impact of father absence on daughters' self-esteem. His master dissertation, "Influence of Absentee Fathers on Daughters' Self-Esteem in Selected Colleges in Ruiru Sub-County, Kiambu County, Kenya," illuminates the challenges faced by young women in the absence of paternal guidance, offering critical insights for both academia and community support.

Celebrating his 25th year in priesthood, Fr. Mark continues to be a beacon of hope and guidance, known for his unwavering dedication to helping individuals navigate life's complexities. His contributions extend beyond the pulpit as an author, with his forthcoming book titled "You're Your Father's Daughter," aiming to inspire and empower individuals with the wisdom gained through his pastoral and academic journey

Reading people

"We are like books. Most people only see the cover, the minority read only the introduction, many people believe the critics. Few will know our contents"

I don't think **people** realize how attentive I am; I'm not dumb, if you think I didn't notice you're greatly mistaken I see everything.

"Once you master reading people nobody can ever play with you."

I read **people.**

I don't just listen to their words

I stare into their faces

I check their body language

"Your body introduce yourself before you can open your mouth"

I peep into their tone

I make note of their use of words.

I hear what they don't say

I interpret their silence

Most importantly. I trust my intuition.

I like people- it's my hobby

"I **simply like pondering what makes people tick."**
People fascinate me more and more; People are a daily adventure if you really go along with them. People are astonishing. There are people with questioning eyes and tense faces. People who are suffering, people in despair and deeply embittered, People who are no longer capable of feeling joy. people who are no longer alive.

What draws me to people

The basis of life is people and how they relate to each other. Our success, fulfillment and happiness depend upon our ability to relate effectively. The best way to become a person that others are drawn to is to develop qualities that we are attracted to in others. When special people touch out live then suddenly, we see how beautiful and wonderful our world can really be. They show us that our special hopes and dreams can take us far by helping us look inward and believe in who we are. They bless us with love and joy through everything they give. when special people touch out lives, they teach us how to live.

People Are Gifts

Some are wrapped very beautifully they are very attractive
    when I first see them
Some come in a very ordinary wrapping paper
Others have been mishandled in the mail
Once in a while there is a special delivery!
Some persons are gifts which come loosely wrapped
Others very tight,
But the wrapping is not the gift
It is easy to make the mistake,
It's amusing when babies do it
Sometimes the gift is very easy to open up
Sometimes I need others to help me.
It is because they are afraid?
Does it hurt?
Maybe they have been opened up before and thrown away

Types of people

People are an interesting but puzzling part of God's Creation. They come in all sizes, shape and personalities.

Some are approachable, warm and friendly, others are aloof, cold and hostile, some are modern, alert, and enthusiastic, others are old fashioned, slow-moving and dull

Some are good-humored, kind and patient, others are cranky, harsh and short-tempered. Some are adventuresome, optimistic and full of fun, others are fearful, pessimistic and sour.

Some are strict but understanding and fair, others are strict, arbitrary and unjust. Some are open to new ideas and ways of doing things, others are close-minded and set in their ways.

Some can see you point of view, when they disagree, others insist that you are wrong, even when you are right. Some challenge, encourage and inspire you, others deter, discourage and dismay you.

Some lead and guide you like a human being. Others drive and force you like an animal. Some know your defects but focus on your good points others see your faults, but are blind to your virtues.

Some always have time to lead a helping hand, others are always too busy to do you a favor, some you will remember forever with gratitude, others you will forgot as soon as possible.

All People matter

"How you treat people is more important than your bank account, education or social status. People will remember your love—or lack of it."

During my second month of college, our lecturer administered a pop quiz. I was a careful student who breezed through the questions until I got to the last one: 'What is the first name of the woman who cleans the school?' Surely this was some sort of prank. I'd seen the cleaning woman numerous times. She was tall, with black hair, and in her fifties, but how would I know her name? I handed in my paper with the last question blank. Just before class concluded, one student inquired if the final question would count toward our quiz grade. 'Absolutely,' the professor said. 'During your professions, you will encounter a lot of individuals. All are noteworthy. They deserve your attention and care, even if that is all you do. Just before class ended, one student inquired if the final question would count toward our quiz grade. 'Absolutely,' the professor said. 'In your professional life, you will encounter a lot of individuals. All are significant. They deserve your attention and care, even if you only smile and say hi. I've never forgotten that lesson. I also learnt that her name was Dorothy.

People Are Mirrors:

A psychologist once asked a group of college students to jot down, in thirty seconds, the initials of the people they disliked. Some of the students taking the test could think of only one person. Others listed as many as fourteen. But the interesting fact that came out of this habit of research was this. Those who disliked the largest number were themselves the most widely dislike.

People with and without gifts.

66 There are only two kinds of people, well, mostly, Receivers and Givers"

I was invited to a wedding, when i reached the hotel, I found two doors written

1. bride relatives

2. Groom relatives

I entered the one written groom relatives and found two more doors

1. ladies

2. men

I went through the one for men only to find two more doors

1. people with gifts

2. people without gift

I went through the one written people without gifts and found myself outside the hotel through the back door at the door it was written

"So, in this time of hard economy you want to just come, eat and drink without any gift, no way"

People are gold

People who immediately reply to your text are not desperate. people who immediately respond to you calls are not desperate, people who are always there for you whenever you need them are not always free or jobless. Maybe they understood what it feels like to be ignored. Maybe they understand what it feels like to be left alone because maybe they were left alone when they needed someone. Maybe the love you. Maybe they have made you, their priority. Never take them for granted. Never lose them. They are gold.

Rejecting people

A guy in a congregational church's choir was unable to sing. Several people suggested that he serve elsewhere, but he persisted to attend the choir. The choir director got desperate and approached the pastor. You need to get the man out of choir, he replied. If you do not, I am going to quit. The choir members are also planning to resign. Please, do something.

The pastor approached the man and suggested he leaves the choir. The man said, "Why should I leave the choir?" He asked. "Well, five or six people have told me you can't sing" "That is nothing," the guy sniffed. "Fifty people have told me you can't preach"

People Are Miracles

"**S**ometimes miracle are just good people with kind hearts"

Wet pants: Come with me to a third-grade classroom.... There is a nine-year-old kid sitting at his desk and all of a sudden, there is a puddle between his feet and the front of his pants are wet. He thinks his heart is going to stop because he cannot possibly imagine how this has happened. It's never happened before, and he knows that when the boys find out he will never hear the end of it. When the girls find out, they'll never speak to him again as long as he lives. The boy believes his heart is going to stop; he puts his head down and prays this prayer, "Dear God, this is an emergency! I need help now! Five minutes from now I'm dead meat."

He looks up from his prayer and here comes the teacher with a look in her eyes that says he has been discovered. As the teacher is walking toward him, a classmate named Susie is carrying a goldfish bowl that is filled with water. Susie trips in front of the teacher and inexplicably dumps the bowl of water in the boy's lap. The boy pretends to be angry, but all the while is saying to himself, "Thank you, Lord! Thank you, Lord!"

Now all of a sudden, instead of being the object of ridicule, the boy is the object of sympathy. The teacher rushes him downstairs and gives him gym shorts to put on while his pants dry out. All the other children are on their hands and knees cleaning up around his desk. The sympathy is wonderful. But as life would have it, the ridicule that should have been his has been transferred to someone else - Susie. She tries to help, but they tell her to get out. You've done enough, you klutz!"

Finally, at the end of the day, as they are waiting for the bus, the boy walks over to Susie and whispers, "You did that on purpose, didn't you?" Susie whispers back, "I wet my pants once too."

People are bridges

Don't underestimate the importance of people in your life. People are the bridges on the highway to your destiny. Relationships are the currency of life; those who invest in them are richly rewarded. Treat every person like they are the missing piece to your life puzzle. At every turning point of your life, God has placed a person waiting to bless you with provisions, instructions, encouragement and direction for your next move. Therefore, honor and value the people that God brings into your life no matter how insignificant they may appear. You cannot move from where you are to where God wants you to be without people. Nobody is too important to need people. Divine blessings, breakthroughs and solutions often come through the least expected people. Even God's greatest gift to humanity, Christ Jesus, came through the person of Mary and He submitted himself to the authority and training of Mary and Joseph for 30 years before he began His ministry. Don't limit your progress. Don't sabotage yourself.

Good people exist

"The world is filled with good people if you can't find one, be one"

A few years ago, I was giving a retreat at a girl' high school in Chicago. One of the girls who came in to talk to me asked: Father, do you remember the terrible fire at our lady of Angels Grammar school. "Oh yes, yes I do" I replied. "Well, I was in that fire:" she said, and I want to tell you about something. They told us that we couldn't go out into the hall because flames were raging in the corridors. We were told to jump out of the windows of our classroom. But I was so small that I couldn't get up on the windowsill. All the other kids in my grade got out. I was the last one still trying to get up on the windowsill, when a large girl who was just about to jump looked back and saw me. She came over to me and lifted me up on the windowsill. Then she pushed me out. As I landed in the schoolyard and looked up, I saw only flames coming from the window. She didn't make it. I will always remember that. It's a memory in me that will never sleep. She died but I have lived she gave her life for.

People can be diabolic

"There is a terrible battle between two wolves going on inside every human heart. One wolf represent evil the other represent good. The one that wins is the one you are feeding".

A gang kidnapped a 3 years old boy at 6pm in kisii-kenya who was said to be playing with other children outside his grandmother's house. The gang held the boy for six hours sending his family in a panic as they searched for the minor's whereabouts. He was later discovered with his eyes gouged out. when the child was rushed to the hospital doctors diagnosed and stated that the boy has lost his capacity to see. The reason behind this gruesome devilish act was to stop the boy from inheriting the family land in the event that his father dies

People may leave bad impression.

What will you be remembered for at the end of life?

One day the famous Jesuit preacher, Fr Bernard Vaughan, was traveling in a train in London. In the compartment there was a tiresome young man who irritated the other passengers at last the young man got out, but just as he reached the station exits, Fr Vaughan rapped on the carriage window and called, "You've left something behind" The young man dashed back, frantically mouthing, "what? What"? through the window as the train began to pull out the station. Fr Vaughan shouted at him, "A very Bad impression"

The people that we are

"People were created to be loved. Thing were created to be used. The reason why the world is in chaos is because things are being loved and people are being used"

"**A**frican are people minded, ie in their view people are more important than either money, wealth or time. For them these things are at the service of the people, they are there to enhance life. They are meant to be at the service of unity and harmony, they are meant to celebrate communion with each other. That is why Africans have extravagant feasts in spite of their poverty."

"The poorer people are, the more they love to celebrate. The festivals of the poorest people in Africa last for several days. They use all their savings on huge feasts. In richer countries we have lost the art of celebration. People go to movies or watch TV or have other leisure activities they go to parties but they do not celebrate." Jean Vanier

"When an African give a party it sizeable party, for parties are for sharing gifts and for showing gratitude for benefits received. Parties are for celebrating unity and for establishing and strengthening relationships. In Africa, people give open parties: everyone is welcome Examples of this are parties for ordinations, burial feasts and ancestral celebrations".

"I once asked a priest who worked for many years in Africa whether he would like to come back in England. Why did he stay on? He replied that he was staying on because as least there he would get a good funeral! He was joking but there was a truth behind what he said. In the so-called underdeveloped world, death is taken seriously. It is an important event, and the community comes to a halt. Everyone attends the funeral. The way you celebrate death is a good indication of how you celebrate life."

Section Two

Aphorism about people

I love quotes because they carry a wealth of wisdom in a single phrase. often, I stumble onto appropriate quotations that are an ideal answer to some of my life's situations and challenges. Every time I find a quote that corresponds to my situation I think, "Thank God I'm not alone." Quates conveys insight that may have taken years to develop in just a few lines. Quotes come from outstanding leaders. Poets. Thinkers and philosophers and deal with numerous life's topics such as people and relationships, how to deal with challenges, the meaning of life, and the values of self-improvement. the necessity of assisting others and the need for strong personality etc.

RESPECT **people** who wear glasses. The paid money to see you

The best thing i ever did was take off the rose-colored glasses and see **people** for who they are, instead of who l want them to be.

We are like books. Most **people** only see the cover, the minority read only the introduction, many people believe the critics. Few will know our contents

How you treat **people** is a ministry and it matters more than any stage or platform you speak preach sing on

I want to motivate and inspire **people** I want someone to look at me and say: "because of you I didn't give up"

If you hate me hate me alone. Don't be out there trying to recruit **people** to hate me

Some **people** want material things. Me. I just want peace. Happy times, and people that love me

People who talk to themselves are more likely to have high IQ

Some people say they care about you and some show they do. Never get them confuse

I love **people** who are highly aware of their worth but are also highly humble and never look down on anybody.

Difficulties will make you understand the difference between l know people and l have **people** in my life

Tell **people** how important they are to you always

My favorite thing is when **people** are just honest with you.

The realest **people** get treated worst, but they win in the end, l promise you that

Some **people** pretend you're a bad person so they don't feel guilty about they thing they did to you.

Difficult times will make you understand the difference between I know people and l have **people.**

Some **people** talk about you because they lost the privilege to talk to you

Stay away **from** people who only see things from their perspective and fail to understand the feelings and thoughts of others

Remember **people** never get jealous of losers

I'm close to very few **people** but those very few people mean everything to me

After certain things happen, you don't feel the same way about **people**, no matter who they are

I pay attention to how **people** treat me. I won't bring it up. I'll just change how l deal with you.

If you knew what was said in your absence, you would stop smiling with a lot of **people**

A lot of **people** are battling depression silently and it's not even about relationships. They just want to survive. May God heal whatever is hurting you.

Some **people** are truly great manipulators. They can lie, cheat, treat you badly and somehow manage to make it all seem like your fault. Don't fall for it. That's just what they do

I was once afraid of people saying: who does she think she is? Now I have the courage to stand up and say: This is who l am.

People respect the money not people

Karma is gonna hit some of you real hard for breaking **people** who had nothing but good intention for you.

People are not showing off. They are genuinely sharing happy moments and achievements. Maybe you are viewing from a jealous point of view

Sometimes you just need a change. From **people,** from you home town, From your career. From your life. Sometimes that's what the heart craves. A new experience. A new love a new job. A new city. And sometimes there's nothing you can do about it. It's one of those things you feel. One of those things that call out to you.

Stop helping ungrateful **people**

The devil will attack you through **people** *you think love you. Watch your circle*

Be careful what you tolerate you are teaching **people** how to treat you.

Don't argue with **people** with no passport they can't even see the world how will they see your point of view

Some **people** are mean and bitter because they had a rough childhood. Some people are kind and caring for the same reason

Position are temporary ranks and tittles are limited but the way you treat **people**, will always be remembered

That's the thing some **people** will completely fuck you over then act as if it was you who did them wrong

It doesn't make you a bad person for wanting the same kind of love you give, you deserve that and more, you deserve **people** who will love you just as much as you love them.

The reason why some **people** are so kind is because the world has been so unkind to them that they don't want other people to feel the way they did.

Keep your distance from **people** who will never admit they are wrong and always try to make you feel like it's all your fault

I never lie because I don't fear anyone. **People** only lie when they are afraid

People who suffer have something to offer to God. when they succeed in enduring their suffering, that is a daily miracle

I don't give up on **people** easily so if I cut you off you really deserve it

People have a lot to say about lives they've never lived

Remember who checks up on you when you get a little quiet. Those are your **people**

Always be ready to survive alone some **people** suddenly change today your important to them, tomorrow you're nothing to them and that's real life

The way I care for **people** makes me wish I had somebody like me in my life

Never stop being a good person just because of bad **people**

Some **people** think I hate them, no bro I don't even think of you

You meet **people** for a reason. Sometimes it's because they're meant to change your life and sometimes it's because you're meant to change theirs

Some **people** aren't good at asking for help because they're so used to being "the helper" Throughout their life they've experience an unbalance give and take so their instinct is usually "I'll figure it out on my own" the self-reliance is all they've ever known

I enjoy myself way too much at home. In my own company, avoiding **people** and minding my business

You have to embrace getting older life is precious and when you've lost a lot of **people** you realize that each day is a gift

Finally entered the phase where I just wants to be around kind **people** who keep it real and love to grow They only people I think are cool now are those who focus on building emotional intelligence, unbinding past trauma and gaining insight through self-awareness

Do not put effort into **people** who don't give it back

True friends are those rare **people** who come to find you in dark places and lead you back to the light

People will act like you're a hard to deal with because you're not easy to fool

Some **people** talk about you because they lost the privilege to talk to you

Stay away **from** people who only see things from their perspective and fail to understand the feelings and thoughts of others

Remember **people** never get jealous of losers

I'm close to very few **people** but those very few people mean everything to me

After certain things happen, you don't feel the same way about **people**, no matter who they are

I pay attention to how **people** treat me. I won't bring it up. I'll just change how l deal with you.

If you knew what was said in your absence, you would stop smiling with a lot of **people**

A lot of **people** are battling depression silently and it's not even about relationships. They just want to survive. May God heal whatever is hurting you.

Some **people** are truly great manipulators. They can lie, cheat, treat you badly and somehow manage to make it all seem like your fault. Don't fall for it. That's just what they do

People respect the money not people

Karma is gonna hit some of you real hard for breaking **people** who had nothing but good intention for you.

People are not showing off. They are genuinely sharing happy moments and achievements. Maybe you are viewing from a jealous point of view

Sometimes you just need a change. From **people,** from you home town, From your career. From your life. Sometimes that's what the heart craves. A new experience. A new love a new job. A new city. And sometimes there's nothing you can do about it. It's one of those things you feel. One of those things that call out to you.

Stop helping ungrateful **people**

Be careful what you tolerate you are teaching **people** how to treat you.

Don't argue with **people** with no passport they can't even see the world how will they see your point of view

Some **people** are mean and bitter because they had a rough childhood. Some people are kind and caring for the same reason

Position are temporary ranks and tittles are limited but the way you treat **people**, will always be remembered

That's the thing some **people** will completely fuck you over then act as if it was you who did them wrong

It doesn't make you a bad person for wanting the same kind of love you give, you deserve that and more, you deserve **people** who will love you just as much as you love them.

The reason why some **people** are so kind is because the world has been so unkind to them that they don't want other people to feel the way they did.

Keep your distance from **people** who will never admit they are wrong and always try to make you feel like it's all your fault

I never lie because I don't fear anyone. **People** only lie when they are afraid

People who suffer have something to offer to God. when they succeed in enduring their suffering, that is a daily miracle

I don't give up on **people** easily so if i cut you off you really deserve it

People have a lot to say about lives they've never lived

Remember who checks up on you when you get a little quiet. Those are your **people**

Always be ready to survive alone some **people** suddenly change today your important to them, tomorrow you're nothing to them and that's real life

The way l care for **people** makes me wish l had somebody like me in my life

People these days don't apologize for doing wrong, rather they blame us for acting how we react

When you help other **people**, you help yourself. Its impossible to not feel great when you do good for other people.

I love **people** who are highly aware of their worth but highly humble too and never look down on anyone.

I don't stress myself to communicate with **people** if you talk to me then okay, if not then okay.

Stop missing **people** who don't even waste a second thinking about you

No matter how good your heart is eventually you have to start treating **people** the way they treat you

Its time to release your grip. Stop holding on to **people** who have already let you go.

I really appreciate when **people** make time for me.

True people cry when your leave, fake people leave when you when you cry

When **people** tell you, you have changed, its only because you stopped acting the way the want you to act.

You are in charge of your own happiness you don't need to wait for other **people**'s permission to be happy

What holds most **people** back isn't the quality of their ideas but their lack of faith in themselves you have to live your life as if you are already where you want to be.

I think I was born irritated. There's no way **people** get on my nerves this much

Never stop being a good person just because of bad **people**

Some **people** think l hate them, no bro I don't even think of you

You meet **people** for a reason. Sometimes it's because they're meant to change your life and sometimes it's because you're meant to change theirs

Some **people** aren't good at asking for help because they're so used to being "the helper" Throughout their life they've experience an unbalance give and take so their instinct is usually "I'll figure it out on my own" the self-reliance is all they've ever known

I enjoy myself way too much at home. In my own company, avoiding **people** and minding my business

You have to embrace getting older life is precious and when you've lost a lot of **people** you realize that each day is a gift

Finally entered the phase where i just want to be around kind **people** who keep it real and love to grow, they only people i think are cool now are those who focus on building emotional intelligence, unbinding past trauma and gaining insight through self-awareness

Do not put effort into **people** who don't give it back

True friends are those rare **people** who come to find you in dark places and lead you back to the light

People will act like you're a hard to deal with because you're not easy to fool

People who cannot love other **people,** start loving money because money is a means to possess things

Sometimes we reduce communication with the **people** we love not because we hate them but because they make us feel like, we are nothing to them.

I found my peace when l realized **people** be at war with themselves and not me.

People can have more than you and still be jealous.

Being nice to **people** who hate you is different level of satisfaction.

Respect **people** who find time for you in their busy schedule, but love people who never look at their schedule when you need them.

Something l learned about **people.** if they, do it once, they'll do it again.

People call it luck when it's actually called alignment. Sacrifice, courage patience and year after year of hard work.

I think l say l love you too much. It's strange how sometimes it startles **people**. But then l remembers that's why I'm here to love and to startle

People will forget what you said, people will forget what you did. But people will never forget how you made them feel

If you hear **people** from my past speak of me keep in mind, they are speaking of a person they don't know anymore

So many **people** these days are too judgmental. l can tell just by looking at them

Cheer to all the **people** with different opinions & we're still friends because we are all adults

I don't distance myself from **people** to teach them a lesson l distance myself because l has finally learned mine

Be kind to unkind **people** they need it most

Notice how **people** change when they don't get what they want from you

Sometime you just have to remove **people** without warning. We're getting too old to be explaining what they already know they're doing wrong

Most **people** don't appreciate what you do for them until you stop doing it.

When two **people** are destined to be together don't worry. Just wait. The love that you seek will come to you in the right time, the right place and with the right person that was meant to love you the way you always wanted

Life is short spend it with **people** who make you laugh and feel loved

Be careful who you share your weakness with, some **people** can't wait for the opportunity to use it against you

It's always the **people** that deserve the best that get the worst

Another problem with having a good heart is that **people** think you're stupid

When **people** expect you to react to their nonsense, remain calm and silent. It's good for the soul and makes them think twice.

Never blame anyone in your life good people give happiness, bad **people** give experiences, worst people give a lesson, best people give memories

The happiest **people** in life are givers not the getters

Sometimes miracles are just good **people** with kind hearts.

The most beautiful things in life are not things. They're **people,** and places, memories and pictures. They're feelings and moments and smiles and laughter

Go thank **people** who've used you. They've made you realized you're not useless:

People always miss you more when they see how much happier you are without them

The most beautiful **people** we have known are those who have known defeat, known suffering, known struggles, known loss, and have found their way out of the depths.

These **people** have an appreciation, sensitivity and an understanding of life that fills them with compassion, gentleness, and deep loving concern. Beautiful people do not just happen

Some **people** will never like you, because your spirit irritates their demons

The most interesting **people** I've ever met have the most colorful pasts, they've lived lives of risk, made bad choices learned lessons, explored, and they're not afraid of being real. Tattered tapestries woven of similar threads, they're my kind of people. My favorite shades of crazy.

Some **people** are so pretty that if they see you looking good, being successful and minding your business. they will bring up some negativity from your past with the sole purpose of trying to steal your joy

One thing I won't do is force **people** to stay in my life. You wanna go, and pretend like l don't exist anymore? Cool, Bye,

Some **people** will never support you simply because you are you. Then there are folks who will support you just because you are you. You only need to discover your folks.

People that introduce you to new ways of thinking and viewing life are really essential.

Sometimes **people** don't want to hear the truth because they don't want to damage their illusions.

Be aware of **people** who continually observe what you are doing but do not congratulate or support you.

The reason why some **people** are so kind is because the world has been so unkind to them that they don't want other people to feel the way they did.

Many **people** will enter your life, but only a few will make a lasting impression.

Don't trust anyone since **people** can change for any reason

Do not blame **PEOPLE** for disappointing you; instead, blame yourself for expecting too much from them.

I used to accept a lot because I didn't want to lose **people**, but now I understand they aren't my people. Set limits.

Some **people** are like M&M's: memories and mistakes

People who claim it is impossible should not interrupt those who are doing it.

I hope that the **people** and things you choose will choose you back.

Accept the fact that everyone will leave you even the **people** who promised to stay.

Once you realize you deserve the best losing **people** from your life doesn't affect you anymore.

Right now, someone you helped is telling **people** you're a bad Person.

I think stupid **people** were put on this planet to test my anger management skill

People will act like you are hard to deal with because you aren't easy to fool.

Serve **people** what you can eat just in case plates are exchanged. This world is too small.

The universe: said: I noticed how your **people** didn't support you so I sent you strangers

Don't stop because the closest **people** to you don't support you, the world is full of strangers ready to root for you.

The worst I ever wish on **people** is that they meet themselves in someone else.

People are scared to say stuff but I'm not and that's why only three people like me.

Be yourself **people** don't have to like you and you son have care.

Let to be okay with **people** not knowing your side of the story you have nothing to prove to anyone.

I like **people** who can sense when to stop talking to me.

Never let **people** think that you can't do without them. Remember there was a time when you didn't know them and you were doing very well.

People raised on love will do anything for you. People raised on survival will do anything to you. Know the difference.

When you**r heart** is pure **people** take advantage of you.

Privacy is power what **people** don't know they can't ruin

Sometimes not matter how nice you are how kind you are how caring you are how loving you are it just isn't enough for some **people**.

The people who wound us get not say in how we clean up the blood

Strong **people** mind discuss ideas, average minds discuss events, weak minds discus people

It's sad how the **people** you were once so close with can become just another stranger you don't know.

When **people** treat you like they don't care, believe them.

Most of the trouble in the world is caused by **people** who want to be important

The right **people** for your soul, hear you differently, show up differently, support you differently, and nourish you differently. That's how you'll know.

I don't do revenge I delete **people**.

Fake has become so acceptable that **people** misunderstand those who stay authentic

Sometimes life will bring **people** into your life and sometimes it will remove them. Trust the process.

Nowadays **people** don't defend what is right, they defend whom they like and benefit from.

There are a lot of jealous **people** with friendly faces

There are so many **people** out there who will tell you that you can't. what you've got to do is turn around and say "watch me"

Work hard until you see yourself on your cousin's status. Families don't like to post broke **people**

Seeing **people** walk out of my life is really painful. I want them to run

Life is too short to waste your time on **people** who don't respect, appreciate and value you

Stay humble because I've seen **people** become what they laughed at

Spend time with **people** who appreciate your presence and value your company

People who have overcome darkness in their life typically have a fire inside them that is almost impossible to extinguish

The right **people** for your soul hear you differently show up differently support you differently and nourish you differently that's how you'll know

Just wanna thank the **people** that get me out the house, invite me to go somewhere and distract me from everything going on in my head.

I hate those **people** who only talk to you when they need something

Focus on **people** who love you, not on people who dont

Be happy in front of **people** who don't like you, it kills them

You are only as pretty as you treat **people**

Never post your achievements post stupid stuff & joke so they'll think you have not future because **people** hate progress seriously

Pay attention to the way you feel around **people**. Energy never lies

Many of life's failures are **people** who did not realize how close they were to success when they gave up

People come and go in your life but the right ones will always stay

Some **people** are upset with you because you're not suffering the way they thought you would be please continuing to disappoint them.

As you evolve you will make a lot of **people** uncomfortable do it anyway

Beautiful things happen when you distant yourself from stupid **people**

Some said a lot of **people** struggle with sleep because sleep require peace, I felt that

Avoiding certain **people** to protect your emotional health is not weakness its wisdom

Success is when you find **people** copying you.

Some **people** are so afraid of abandonment that they're recreating their own abandonment

Stay away from **people** who only notice your results not your efforts

People grow when they are loved well. If you want to help others heal, love them without an agenda

Today l am grateful for all the people that are loving and kind to me

The reason why some **people** are so kind is because the world has been so unkind to them that they don't want other people to feel the way they did.

Not caring what **people** think and growing at you own pace is self-care

I have seen beauty in **people** who were called ugly and I've seen the devil in the most angelic faces

People will come and go in life, but the person in the mirror will be there forever. so be good to yourself

For the **people** who try to bring me down you made me stronger than l was.

The less you respond to negative **people** the more peaceful your life will become

Never let your feelings go too deep **people** can change anytime

If l knew then what l know now. I would've avoided a lot of **people**

Some **people** are not your friends they are just scared to be your enemy

The hardest pill l swallowed was realizing l meant nothing to **people** that meant a lot to me

I don't think **people** understand how observant l am. Like I'm really not a fool.

Some **people** take you for granted then later realize that you were rare

My love language is when **people** say they'll be there for you and then actually prove it

After certain things happen you don't feel the same way about **people** no matter who they are.

It's a little embarrassing that after 45 years & study. The best advice l can give **people** is to be a little kinder to each other.

Avoid taking **people** for granted because those who love you deeply can reach their limits

There is nothing worse than **people** who only see things from their point of view and refuse to try to understand anything from someone else's perspective

If you live for **people's** acceptance you'll die from their rejections.

Stop telling **people** more than they need to know.

The person you don't love is checking on you every day but the **people** you want in life are ignoring you every day.

Be nice to **people**. But don't lend then money, they won't pay back

Cheer to all the **people** with different opinions & we're still friends because we are all adults

Some of the most generous **people** have not money. some of the wisest people have no education. Some of the kindest people were hurt the most

I don't distance myself from **people** to teach them a lesson l distance myself because l has finally learned mine

Day by day, I'm training my heart to accept disappointment even from **people** l love

When **people** know they did you wrong. They avoid you

Be proof that good **people** with no hidden agendas still exist.

There's a special place in hell for **people** who take too long to reply

Irony is **people** who don't change their underwear want to change the world

I have smiled at **people** who have said the most terrible things about me and they think l don't know

People with big hearts attract the most draining disloyal and disrespectful people

When you don't move like everybody else its bothers **people**

I love the **people** l have in my life right now. I don't have many but they're all real ones and I' m forever grateful

My problem is... I expect me out of **people**

The most beautiful **people** we have known are those who have known struggle, know loss, and have found their way out of the depths. beautiful people do not just happen.

Accept that you are not important to some **people** and move on

Some **people** ruin the happiness in others because they can't find their own.

Successful **people** are not gifted they just work hard, then succeed on purpose

There are so many **people** out there who will tell you that you can't. what you've got to do is turn around and say "watch me"

Be careful what you tell **people**. A friend today could be an enemy tomorrow

When **people** know they did wrong. They avoid you.

Keep you distance from **people** who will never admit they are wrong and always try to make you feel like it is all your fault.

Don't chase **people** instead chase a better life and a better you

The less **people** you chill with, the less problems you deal with.

When people treat you like they don't care believe them.

You glow differently when you have good **people** with good intentions in your life.

I can't stress how important the **people** are who check-in to see if you're okay, when they notice you've been quiet . That's real friends

I've learnt the painful lesson that it's ok to keep some **people** in my heart, but not in my life. Accepting that they are a part of my history, but not my destiny

Angry **people** want you to see how powerful they are. loving people want you to see how powerful you are

Understanding is deeper than information, there are **people** who know us, but very few who understand us.

Never regret being a good person to the wrong **people**. Your behavior says everything about you. And their behavior says enough about them.

Day by day, I'm training my heart to accept disappointment even from **people** I love

Be yourself **people** don't have to like you and you don't have to care.

There are going to be **people** that don't fit in anymore. And that's okay

I hate when **people** can't see the wrong in their actions but see the wrong in yours

The happiest **people** don't' have the best of everything they just make the best of everything.

I wish I had met certain **people** earlier, later, or never at all.

People can fabricate stories about you, ruin your reputation, and damage your personality, but they will never be able to take away your good acts. Because, regardless of how they characterize you. Those who know you best will always admire you.

More **people** than I visit my past. Baby, I'm not living there anymore. I closed the deal on the entire structure.

some **people** are anticipating your collapse. Let those who are waiting for you to give up waiting indefinitely.

Not because you don't care, but rather because they don't, you have to give up on **people** sometimes.

The most misinterpreted power move you will ever make is allowing **people** to be wrong about you or a scenario while maintaining your composure and attention.

Some **people** never really appreciate what you have to offer until they see you in action at another table.

There are a lot of jealous **people** with friendly faces be careful

Special are the **people** who make you believe that you're special

The **people** who have the biggest impact on your life stay for the shortest time

I respect **people** that use their pain as a guideline for how not to treat other

If you have to insult other **people** to make yourself feel better I feel so bad for you.

The **people** who come running to hug you after you haven't seen them in a while are my favorite people

I love reading motivational post from **people** I know are toxic in real life

Keep **people** in your life that truly love you, motivate you encourage you, inspire you, make you happy. if you have people who do none of the above let them go

Sometimes you just need to distance yourself from **people** if they care, they'll notice if they don't you know where you stand with them.

Sit with **people** who protect your name in your absence

Take care of the **people** you love but take even better care of the people that love you.

Be careful who you build with, because **people** will use you for the foundation and finish the structure with someone else

You've got to find **people** who love like you do.

Always be ready to survive alone. some **people** suddenly change. Today you are important to them, tomorrow you are nothing to them and that's real life.

People ask you what you do for a living so that they can calculate the level of respect to give you.

Know you place in **people**'s lives and act accordingly. it's not pride, its self-respect. Two things you don't fight for. True love and true friends. They come naturally

Things end, **people** change and you know what life goes on.

Temporary **people** give permanent lessons

I am exactly where l wants to be. At home, avoiding **people.**

Stop explaining yourself and telling **people** everything. You owe no one any explanations of what you do. Your life is yours not theirs

Don't' blame **people** for disappointing you. Blame yourself for expecting to much from them.

I have smiled at **people** who said the most terrible things about me and they think l don't know.

Sometimes we lose **people** because we over love them

There are some **people** who always seem angry and continuously look for conflict, walk away, they battle they are fighting isn't with you. It is with themselves

You have no idea what **people** are dealing with in their personal lives so just be nice. It's that simple.

Don't waste time on revenge the **people** who hurt you will eventually face their own karma

Sometimes in life you have to accept the truth. And stop wasting time on the wrong **people.**

I spent a lot of time with myself, **people** call it loneliness I call it self-love.

Even when you're having difficulties, you never realize how many **people** you're motivating.

There will come a moment in your life when some **people** will wish they had not treated you badly. Believe me. It will undoubtedly arrive.

Exercise caution. **People** begin to love your hand rather than your heart when you give them too much.

You are loved by certain **people.** There are those that enjoy your company. There are many that adore your services. Recognize the distinction.

These days, **people** defend those who they like and who helps them rather than what is right.

Stay away from **people** who appreciate only the wealthy.

In all honesty, nobody is pain-free, thus you should never undervalue someone else's suffering. Simply said, some **people** are more adept than others at disguising it.

I will reiterate. Drama is started by unhappy **people.**

People that consistently undermine your confidence and self-esteem are aware of your potential, even if you are not. They borrow your money with a grin and return it with an attitude.

I've smiled at **people** who have said the worst things about me, and they believe I don't know.

How you treat **people** is a ministry, and it is more important than the stage or platform from which you speak. Preach or sing on.

Fasting from **people** negative conversation and poor mindset is top tier

For **people** who attempted to pull me down. You made me stronger than I was.

Someone said a lot of **people** struggle with sleep because sleep require peace l felt it

People borrow your money with smile and return it with attitude.

People believe that intimacy is about sex. But closeness is about the truth. When you discover you can tell someone the truth, show them who you are, and stand naked in front of them, and their answer is. You are safe with me; this is intimacy.

Chemistry between **people** is the most powerful science of all.

Some **people** just hate you because they can't figure out how God is still blessing you after what they said about you.

Life is too short to tolerate nonsense. Cut out negativity ignore gossip, and let go of fake **people**

You never know how much **people h**ates you until what's in the heart comes out of their mouth.

Don't ignore the things **people** say. Especially when they say evil things against you.

Hearts are being revealed in this season. **People** you thought were for you will be exposed.

Don't be afraid to do something just because you are scared of what **people** will say about you. People will always judge you anyway.

Listen to what **people** do no say.

People aren't ignoring you; they're busy with their lives, instead of feeling ignored, get busy with yours

Never force **people** to choose you.

Beautiful souls recognize beautiful souls. Keep being genuine. Your **people** will find you.

People will start hating you when they cannot control you. Remember that.

When you start seeing your worth, you will find it harder to stay around **people** who don't

Be careful what you tolerate, you are teaching **people** how to treat you,

It's important to find **people** who make you realize there's nothing wrong with being who you are.

The problem is **people** are being hated when they are real, and are being loved when they are fake.

Don't be too humble, don't be too rude, just treat **people** according to their attitude

You will embrace getting older. Life is precious and when you've lost a lot of **people**, you will realize each day is a gift.

I don't care what **people** think of me. I enjoy my life with my own rules,

Never be afraid to treat **people** the way they treat you.

Life is too short to tolerate nonsense, cut out negativity ignore gossip, and let go of fake **people**

It's not my job to be likeable. It's my job to be myself. The right **people** will gravitate toward you.

Know your place in **people's** lives and act accordingly. It's not pride, its self-respect.

Love your life. Take pictures of everything. Tell **people** you love them. Talk to random strangers, do things that you're scared to do, so many of us die and no one remembers a thing we did. Take your life and make it the best story in the world. Don't waste it.

Be yourself no matter what other **people** think. God made you the way you are for a reason. Besides an original is always worth more than a copy.

It doesn't matter if **people** are for you or against you: always back yourself like your life depends on it, because it does.

Don't chase **people**. Be an example. Attract them. Work hard and be yourself. The people who belong in your life will come and find you and stay. Just do your thing.

Who cares if they stop talking to you? You breathe air, not **people**

It is usually futile to try to talk facts and analysis to **people** who are enjoying a sense of moral superiority in their ignorance

Some **people** are going to reject you, simply because you shine too bright for them. And that is okay keep shinning

People today say they love you Just to be saying they love you. The next time a person tells you they love you, ask them to give you 5 reasons why they love you. If they do, they will be able to give you those reasons. You will learn to a lot from their answer or their silence.

Appreciate what you have. There are **people** who pray for the things we take for granted

People who have been single for too long are the one hardest to love. They are have become so used to being single, independent and self-sufficient that it takes something extraordinary to convince them that they need you in their life.

If someone really loves you no matter how many **people** they meet, their feelings for you wouldn't change. A real lover can't be stolen

The universe loves grateful **people**. The more grateful you are, the more you get to be grateful about it. It's that simple

Sometime when **people** you love hurt you the most. It's better to remain quiet because if our love wasn't enough. Do you really think your words will matter?

It's during the toughest time of your life that you'll see the true colors of the **people** who say they care about you. Notice who sticks around and who doesn't and be grateful to those who leave you, for they have given you the room to grow.

You're over here doubting yourself while so many **people** are intimidated by your potential

I admire **people** who choose to shine even after all the storm they have been through.

Always be ready to survive alone. some **people** suddenly change. Today your important to them. Tomorrow you are nothing to them and that's life

You become unstoppable when you work on things that **people** can't take away from you. Things like your mindset. Character and personality

Know you place in **people's** lives and act accordingly. it's not pride, its self-respect. Two things you don't fight for.... True love and true friends. They come naturally.

Some **people** will only love you as much as they can use you. Their loyalty ends where the benefits stop

People will come and go in life, but the person in the mirror will be there forever so be good to yourself

People don't abandon people they love; People abandon people they were using

People avoid uncomfortable conversation to "keep the peace". But peace isn't the goal of the relationship. Love is. And when we love someone, we have the hard conversation

Everything heals and grows when it is loved well. **People** too

There are a lot of jealous **people** with friendly faces. Be careful

Beauty isn't the way you hold yourself. It's how you treat **people.** The way you love. Its self-acceptance Beauty is in your soul

The **people** who are meant to be in your life will always gravitate back towards you no matter how far they wander

When **people** are rude, harsh, critical or argumentative, recognize it not really about you and resist the urge to react emotionally. Don't allow their behavior to dictate your mood or steal your peace.

People who love you always come back to you.

There are **people** who have money and people who are rich

Amazing how some **people** simply disappear from your life

One day the **people** that didn't believe in you will tell everyone how they met you.

When you fly high, **people** will throw stones at you. Don't look down. Just fly higher so the stones won't reach you.

I think stupid **people** were put on this planet to test my anger management skills.

People say "never give up" but sometimes giving up is the best option because you realize you're wasting your time

I don't even know why **people** take me so seriously, I never even know what I'm saying

There comes a time in life when you walk away from all the drama and **people** who create it. Surround yourself with people who make you laugh, forget the bad and focus on the good. Love the peoplewho treat you right. Pray for the ones who don't life is too short to be anything but happy. Falling down is part of life getting up is living.

The problem with closed minded **people** is that their mouth is always open

Undisputed fact: The only three **people** a woman attentively listens to and obeys sincerely and do exactly as they say is a doctor and the pastor and photographer otherwise if you're neither of the three sit down and be strong.

I hate **people** who say women love money was Judas a woman? Tsiuuuuuup

Do you ever sit down and think about **people** who passed away and reality hits you like, "they really gone forever"?

Never forget 3 types of **people** in your life. 1) who helped you in difficult times 2) who left you in you in your difficult times 3) who put you in difficult times.

God uses ordinary **people** to do extraordinary things for his glory

Know this: some **people** will not hear you regardless how much, how loud how truthful how loving or how profound you speak. Wish them well

If you don't work hard, you will be calling successful **people** devils worshippers and prostitute for the rest of your life.

Spend time praying for **people** instead of talking about them.

I finally realized it **people** are prisoner of their own phones. That's why they are called cell phones

When someone lends you money, it doesn't mean they have a lot. It means they thought you needed it more than them. so learn to return **people's** money with the same energy and smile you borrowed it

Remember this: Right **people** will never get tired of you.

We feel we can't survive sometimes dreams are shattered. Friendship may fall apart. Love ones may hurt us. Finances may worry us. Sickness may overtake us. We may even lose **people** we love. But God will always be there to guide us through even the toughest of times Never lose faith. Hold onto hope. Trust in God always.

People think that intimacy is about sex, but intimacy is about truth. When you realize you can tell some your truth, when you can show yourself to them when you stand in front of them and their response is "you're safe with me" that's intimacy.

Hear me when I tell you.**: people** who ignore you until it suit them to talk to you, are not worth your friendship or your time!

Too many **people** think the grass is green somewhere else. But the grass is green where you water it.

Some **people** are not speaking to you because they know they owe you an apology

Don't expect **people** to be there for you just because you're always there for them not everyone has the same heart as you.

Drive carefully on this road called "life" because **people** will switch lanes on you without a signal.

If you're around **people** who can confidently speak up when your behavior is impacting them negatively, it means they have respect for themselves, and it means they are teaching you how to love them because they value you enough to keep you in their lives.

Don't joke with this prayer: God connect me with people who matter to my purpose

Respectfully: I don't go above and beyond for **people** anymore. I meet you as far as you meet me. I speak as much as you speak to me. Include you as much as you include me

I don't have pride. I just don't like bothering **people,** that's why I don't text first

I don't hurt **people** with a lie, i kill them with truth.

I didn't change l just started treating **people** like the treat me.

I don't think there's anything more beautiful than having **people** in your life who make your feel emotionally safe. Who welcome you into a judgement free zone? People who possess the maturity to calmly speak about any troubling or difficult topic that may arise. That's special

Sometimes i feel bad for not checking up on **people,** but then I realize the phone works both ways and there aren't nobody checking up on me

I was once a **people** person. But the people ruined that for me. Now I'm a coffee person.

Some **people** think I hate them, no bro i don't even think of you.

I hope everyone loses their attachment to **people** who don't reciprocate their energy,

Don't be disappointed if **people** refuse to help you. Remember the words of Einstein "I am thankful to all those who SAID NO, Because of them I did it MYSELF".

I no longer listen to what **people** say, I just watch what they do. Behavior never lies

When the right **person** hugs you. It's like medicine. I'm so grateful for the few people in my life who are good for my soul

The only **people** who deserve to be in your life are the ones who treat you with love, kindness, and respect.

I don't like when **people** touch me i gotta really like you for you to touch me.

Some people are investments and some **people** are bills.

There will be **people** who deny your reality because they are not willing or able to be honest about their own

The world is full of kind **people.** If you can't find one be one

Never let your feelings go too deep **people** can change anytime

Maturity is when you don't force **people** to choose you.

Don't blame **people** for disappointing you, blame yourself for expecting too much from them.

Don't tell **people** your plans, show your results

Never hate jealous **people.** They are jealous because they think you are better than them.

When you don't move like everyone else it bothers **people.**

A time will come in your life when some **people** will regret why they treated you wrong. Trust me, it will definitely come.

Some **people** visit my past more than I do. I don't live there anymore baby. I sold the whole building.

The crazy thing about **people** who don't like you. They watch everything you do.

Be proof that good **people** with no hidden agendas still exist.

Worry about your character, not your reputation. Your character is who you are. Your reputation is who **people** think you are.

Some **people** want material things me. I just want peace, happy times and people that love me

Be yourself **people** don't have to like you and you don't have to care.

The most genuine **people** get treated worst sometimes, but win in the end, i promise you that.

The biggest lesson learned this year is probably to not give so much of yourself to **people** who will not do the same to you

Sometimes I wish **people** could drink their words and realize how bitter they taste.

Why can't **people** see the good things in front of them?

Most of us spend out entire lives trying to earn the acceptance of others when all we need to do is accept ourselves and allow **people** to love us for who we really are.

Notice how **people** change when they don't get what they want from you.

Know your worth. **People** will try to give you less than you deserve

I am different and it has cost me many **people**, but I am always myself. It's in better to lose others that to lose yourself.

The older you get the more you realize some relationship end because they are temporary **people** who taught you permanent lessons. It's crazy how peaceful life becomes when you start learning, healing, and raising the bar to who has access to your body heart, and soul

I don't wish bad upon nobody but you reap what you sow in life, You don't treat **people** like shit and love a happy life

Stick with the **people** who saw your potential while everyone counted you off

Now I'm not surprised when **people** leave. I'm actually surprised when they stay.

Sometimes you just need to distance yourself from **people**. If they care, they'll notice. If they don't, you know where you stand

I started treating **people** how they treat me... Now everybody's mad.

There are two **people** in a relationship. The loyal one and the one who has learned to take the advantage of the loyal one.

Why is it that...All the **people** you actually want to be around, live nowhere near you

Only 3 types of people tell the truth. 1) Kids. 2) The drunk. 3) The angry.

Apparently, when you treat **people** the same way they treat you, they get offended

The world is filled with kind **people** if you can't find one, be one.

To all the **people** who are loving and kind to me. Thank you for the sunshine you bring into my life.

Sometimes the **people** you want as part of your story are only meant to be a chapter.

People who have dealt with abandonment issues are precious human beings. They don't' like allowing people in: they fear that you'll get close, use them and abandon them. They value relationships at the deepest level due to the desire to be loved and connected. However, its only too much to someone who isn't ready for an intense love affair. They also will never forget that time where you were there for them, those voids have defined their life. Value and cherish those who have been abandoned

I used to be afraid of losing **people** until I realized most of them were never really down for me anyway even though my loyalty and love for them ran deep they couldn't care less, so instead d of losing them I fell back and watched them lose me

People like you are rare to find. Never forget your worth

Thank **people** for the small things they do that make you feel loved

The crazy thing about the **people** that don't like you, they watch everything you do

Angry **people** want you to see how powerful they are loving people want you to see how powerful you are

A little reminder you are allowed to talk about what they did to you and how it hurt you it does not matter how they feel about talking about it because if they wanted **people** to think better of them, they should have been better.

Stay connected to **people** who bring out the best in you and help you grow

When **people** can't control you, they try to control how **people** view you.

After certain things happen you don't feel the same way about **people** no matter who they are

You don't need **people** to spell out their feelings for you. Just watch how they act and you'll know for sure,

Do you know that some **people** hate you because somebody lied to them about you?

People who suddenly stop talking to you, usually start talking about you.

Be the thing you loved most about the **people** who are gone.

Grateful for all the wonderful things in my life and the amazing **people** who surround me

No matter what **people** think of you always keep singing your own song.

I don't care what anyone says good **people** get tired being good to ungrateful **people.**

Its ok to outgrow **people** who don't grow

The best weight to lose is the weight of other **people's** opinion

Don't let Instagram fool you. There are **people** with only 10 likes and have plenty of friends and people with 1000's of likes that incredibly lonely. There are couples that appear extremely happy yet are dysfunctional relationship. There are girls who over-expose their bodies yes feel the most insecure. There are guys who flaunt lavish lifestyles yes are struggling with debts. Things aren't always what they appear to be. Social media has created an outlet for narcissistic behavior, where self-worth is determined by the number of likes received. Appearances are just that, appearances

Someone said "If you look at **people** in your circle and you don't get inspired, then you don't have a circle. You have a cage"

Sometimes quiet **people** do have a lot to say. They're just being careful about who they up to

Stop expecting you from others **people.**

No matter what **people** think of you always keep sing your own song

People who are good from heart will always be rough at speaking out.

Let's heal so we can stop accidentally hurting **people** we want to love because we are projecting our own wounds on to them.

If you care what other **people** think your will always be the prisoner

No matter how educated, rich or cool you believe you are. How you treat **people** ultimately tells all. Integrity is everything

We hurt our own feelings by thinking we mean more to **people** than we really do.

Unhappy **people** always try to make others as miserable as they are

I grew up to understand that **people** don't always build walls to keep others out. It's done out of a necessity to protect whatever is left within

Some **people** want it to happen some wish it would happen others make it happen.

Don't take things so **people.** What people say about you is reflection of them, not you.,

Another problem with having a good heart is that **people** think you're stupid

Did you know? Your shoes are the first thing **people** subconsciously notice about you. wear nice shoes

You glow differently when you have good **people** with good intentions in your life

Teach your heart to accept disappointments even from **people** you love.

Sometimes the only **people** who truly understand where you come from are those who have been there.

You seriously have no idea what **people** are dealing with in their personal life so just be nice it's that simple

There's nothing louder than silence between two **people** who used to love each other

I fight every day in ways most **people** don't understand

Most of the enemies you have are **people** you once helped

Being good is also a mistake nowadays **people** think you are fake

Usually, the **people** who make the biggest impact in your life stay for the shortest time

I can't even make a straight line using a ruler, why do **people** expect so much from me

There are two types of **people** in the world: 1) People who understand and appreciate sarcasm 2) Idiot

People who are at war with themselves can't give peace

I like offending **people** because 1 think people who get offended should be offended

I am at a point where 1 don't even care about **people** who like me If you like Me Cool, if you don't like me okay

You don't need a reason to help **people.**

It's like most **people** don't want to talk with attractive ladies.

Do you know what i have noticed? Complete stranger is more inclined to help you succeed than **people** you know.

Listen to the advice of older **people.** Not because they're right but because they have the most experience.

People like to bring up your past when your present and future look better than theirs

That's the problem with some **people**, if you trust them, they start proving you wrong

People without a sense of humor stay from my write ups and stop bitching

People will push you away and say that you gave up on them

The sad truth is that so many **people** are in love not together and so many people are together and no in love

You can't change how **people** feel about you so don't try just live your live and be happy

When you die **people** may cry and beg for you to come back, but when you're here they don't even show they care about you.

I have never seen God but l knows how l feel its people like you who make him so real

One day the **people** that didn't believe in you will tell everyone how they met you

There are few things the ego delights in more than correcting **people's** mistakes

Some **people** cry not because they are weak but because they've been strong for far too long

Don't blame **people** for disappointing you blame yourself for expecting too much from them

I think the scariest thing in this world is that you never really know what **people's** intentions are with you.

Most **people** need love and acceptance more than they advise,

Even my phone battery lasts long the love of **people** these days

People rarely need advice they want to be listened to heard and validated

Always be ready to be alone. Some **people** suddenly change. Today you are important to them tomorrow you are not and that's real life.

There is a special place in heaven for **people** who know the art of appreciation

Compliment **people**, magnify their strength not their weakness

Some **people** feel like a small pebble lost on the immensity of the Grand Canyon, but no matter how insignificant we judge ourselves to be we can be greatly used by God.

People don't fake depression the fake being okay! Remember that and be kind.

I like straightforward **people** they 're not afraid to tell you what's up.

The problem with life is by the time we realized we're blessed with some good **people** in our life with whom we share some of the best memories they either get busy or leave

People disappear quickly when you show them that you need them

Notice the amazing **people** in your life

Stop making **people** to think you can't live without them. Remind them that there was a time you did not know them and you were alright. Nobody is God's secretary or assistant

Don't admire **people** too much they might disappoint you

Imagine how many **people** dislike you because they never hear you side of the story

What **people** say about you is a reflection of them and not you.

Why is it that generous **people** find it hard to ask for help when they are going through tough time?

A positive attitude may not solve all your problems but it annoys enough **people** to make it worth the effort

May be **people** who make you doubt yourself a little are actually your best friends

I don't even feel like a "friend" I feel more like an option or someone they run to when they need something.

Yes, I see there are **people** who say don't trust strangers. I suggest them to drive their own trains and fly own planes

The best feeling comes when you realize you're perfectly happy without the **people** you thought needed the most.

There are a lot of **people** who call you by your name, but there is only one person who can make it sound so special.

Some **people** are going to love you no matter what you do, And some people will never love you no matter what you do.

If **people** could see the faces I make when I read their up status/ updated they would probably unfriendly.

I just like thinking about what makes **people** tick

There is always a reason why you meet **people**. Either you need them to change your life or you're the one that will change theirs

People never realized they lost something good until they see someone else with it.

Never get into fights with ugly **people** because they have nothing to lose

I hate the type of **people** who don't notice you when you're ignoring them.

People don't care how much you know until they know how much you care.

The best thing about **people** who love you is that you don't have to impress them.

Most **people** don't what to hear these but real relationships that last involve a lot of forgiveness. You have to accept the fact that your partner isn't perfect and will hurt you, disappoint you and upset you. You have to figure out if you're willing to go through ups and downs with them.

Don't worry when you have a bad day remember there are people who have their ex's name tattooed.

The **people** who hide their feelings usually care the most

The best way to hide something from black **people** is to put it in a book.

Not everyone will make it to your future some **people** are just passing through to teach you a lesson

Nobody owes us anything that is what makes **people** who care about us so unique.

The sweetest hearted **people** are the most mistreated people

Sometimes you are just too real for **people** they're not use to that

Sometimes two **people** have to fall apart to realize how much they need to fall back together.

When l was young l admired intelligent **people.** As l grows older l admires kind people.

Broken **people** are always the ones who try to fix up others

My favorite thing is when **people** remember little things, I told them: Like you actually listened to me thank you.

Pay attention to how **people** act when you're on good terms

I'm slowly learning not to let my happiness depend on other **people.**

Stay away from **people** who have benefited from you but act as if you have never done anything good for them

People are even scared to check on you because you beg a lot

The most memorable **people** in life will be the ones who loved you when you weren't very lovable

Only few things as scary as **people** who suddenly start acting all nice to you.

There will always be **people** who tell you you're beautiful and there would also be someone who'll make you feel it.

God doesn't give the **people** you want he gives the people you need. To help you, to hurt you, to leave you, to love you and to make you the person you were meant to be.

People will really care for you will always keep enough margin for your errors

There is special place in hell for **people** who take too long to reply

Irony is **people** who don't change their underwear everyday want to change the world.

The **people** who go out of their ways for you expecting nothing in return. Thank you.

Sometime l push **people** away just to see if they care enough to make an effort to stay in my life. And sometimes they really surprise me by walking away.

In life there some **people** you're going to have to lose in order to find yourself

People may have spoken negative things about you but the good news is people don't determine your destiny. You are who God says you are.

I want to motivate and inspire **people.** I want people to look at me and say: *"Because of you l didn't give up"*

People who tell me there is no God are like a six-year-old saying that there is no such thing as passionate love. They just haven't experience it

On the way to success, you will find plenty of jealous **people**

People who sneeze in the palms of their hands rubbing it all over should be given a punch on the face.

People will smile at you when you make eye contact with them are my favorite kind of people.

Train your heart to accept disappointment even when they come from **people** you trusted with your heart

Sometimes the **people** whom you avoid are the one who actually want to help you.

Some **people** are so beautiful that they have nothing to do with looks

Some **people** treat life like a slot machine putting as little as possible while hoping for the jackpot

Some **people** are very angry at you because you are not suffering, the way they expected you to. May God keep disappointing them.

You won't stay on top if you're mistreating the **people** who were there before anyone ever heard your name.

You think you know **people** and they surprise you.

Cute how **people** start noticing what you did for them after you are out of their lives

The **people** you dislike are in your life for a reason they are there to teach you something about yourself.

Family isn't blook. It's the **people** who have your back

The worst distance between two **people** is misunderstanding

Notice the **people** who are happy for your happiness and sad for your sadness. They're the one who deserve a place in your heart

Don't take advantage of **people** who love you.

Be careful who let on your ship because some people will sink the whole ship, just because they can't be captain.

Sometimes **people** don't want to hear the truth because they don't want their illusions destroyed

I didn't change l just started treating **people** they way they treat me.

Always stay true to yourself because there are few **people** who will always be true

Sometime it's not the song that makes you emotional, it the **people** and the things that come to your mind when you hear it.

People who have done you wrong will always think your posts are about them.

Sometimes you put walls up not to keep **people** out, but to see who cares enough to break them down.

People are doubting how far you can go, go so so far that you can't hear them anymore.

Sometimes l wish **people** could drink their own words and realized how bitter they taste

You define your own life don't' let other **people** write your script.

Sometimes l just agrees with **people** so that they can stop talking to me.

In reality other **people** liking you is a bonus, you liking them is the real prize.

Work so hard one day **people** who rejected you will search for you in Google.

In life it's important to know when to stop arguing with **people** and simply let them be wrong.

Never force **people** to choose you

I love **people** who gossip behind my back. That's exactly where they belong behind my back.

When you help other **people**, you help yourself, it's impossible to not feel great when you do good for other people.

People raised on love see things differently than those raised on survival

Be positive that negative **people** don't want to be near you.

Always be ready to survive alone some **people** suddenly change. Today you are important to them, tomorrow you are nothing to them and that's real life.

The hardest pill l swallowed was realizing l meant nothing to **people** that meant a lot to me.

Sometimes you just need to distance yourself from **people**. If they care they'll notice. If they, don't you know where you stand.

Notice how **people** change when they don't get what they want from you.

Let people lose you. Let **people** be wrong about you. Learn to leave well enough alone. Often the greatest peace is not found in correcting others. It's found in correcting yourself, accepting the lessons and knowing when to walk away.

No need to cut **people** off. Just grow, they will fall off.

Teach your heart to accept disappointment even from **people** you love.

Know your worth and stop giving **people** discounts

Some **people** are better for you from a distance.

You become unstoppable when you work on things **people** can't take away from you. Things like your mindset, character, personality, transparency, your entire being.

I'm close to very few **people** but those few people mean everything to me

There are rare **people** who will show up at the right time, help you through the hard times and stay into your best times. Those are keepers

I like to hang out with **people** who make me forget to look at my phone

The older l get the more l accept that some **people** will stay the same and l do not have to be the fixer.

Life is like a party. You invite **people,** some leave early, some stay all night, some laugh with you and some at you. But in the end, there are few who stay to help you clean up the mess these people are your true friends. They are the only ones who matter.

People might not always be able to help you the way you want but they did the way they could, appreciate it.

There are two types of **people** that come into our lives, they are temporary and permanent. Temporary people come to teach you lessons like hurt, pain. Selfishness, heartbreak dishonesty and disloyalty Permanent **people** come into your heart; they are the ones that give you strength confidence and loyalties. Real love is found here. The truth is you need the two, because one teaches value over the other.

People will borrow money with a smile, then return it with an attitude.

Learning how to leave **people** alone and go on with your life is needed skill, you must master it.

Never trust words. Some **people** have sugar on their lips but venom in their hearts

Those who look for bad in **people** will surely find it.

The **people** you always remember are the one who made you feel love when you were at your lowest.

Be happy with the little that you have. There are **people** with nothing that still manage to smile.

I don't know how **people** can fake an entire relationship l can't even fake hello to someone l doesn't like

Always be there for **people** who matter the most to you.

It's sad how **people** can forget about you until they want something from you.

You can be friends with **people** for years and it could take years to realize they were never your friends

Sometime in life you have to accept the truth and stop wasting time on the wrong **people.**

Accept that you are not important to some **people** and move on.

People have a lot to say about lives they've never lived

If **people** don't make an effort to be in your life, don't try to be in their it's not worth it.

I am aware that l is less than some **people** prefer me to be. But most **people** are unaware that l am so much more than what they see.

Sometimes temporary **people** teach you permanent lessons

Some **people** have food, but can't eat. Other can eat but they have no food. But for you, you have both if you're grateful Thank God. Amen

People come and go in your life, but the right one will always stay.

Good things happen in your life when you surround yourself with positive **people.**

We are often let down by the most trusted **people** and loved by the most unexpected one. Some make us cry for things we haven't done, while other ignore our faults and just see out smile. Some leave us when we need the most, while some stay with us even when we ask them to leave. The world is a mixture of people. We just need to know which hand to shake and which hand to hold! After all that's life learning to hold on and learning to let go.

Understand this: the insults, judgments and shade **people** attempt to throw your way are actually projections of their own insecurities and are absolutely irrelevant to you and your life

Surround yourself with **people** who love your life and add it.

Some **people** are beautiful not in looks, not in what they say, just in what they are.

If you feel pain, you're alive. if you feel other **people's** pain, you're a human being.

Nobody watches you harder than **people** that don't like you. Give them a show.

People know your name not your story. They've heard about what you've done but not what you've been through. So, take their opinion of you with a grain of salt. In the end, it's not what others think of you but what you think about yourself that counts

The only people worthy to be in your life are those that help you through hard time and laugh with you after the hard times pass.

Silly me expecting too much from **people** again.

People come people go. That's life

If you have the chance to make a **people** happy. Just do it. some people are struggling silently. Maybe you act of kindness can make their day.

I appreciate **people** who don't give up on me

Everyone in your life is going to hurt you; you just have to figure out which **people** are worth the pain.

People will provoke you until they until they bring out your ugly side, then play victim when you go there.

People with good heart are always unlucky in relationship

Be happy in front of **people** who don't like you, it kills them.

People will lie directly to your face then get mad at you because you don't trust them.

People who have overcome darkness in their life typically have a fire inside them that is almost impossible to extinguish

Focus on people who love you, not on **people** who don't

I hate those **people** who only talk to you when they need something.

Choose your circle wisely some **people** will judge and criticize your changes, while others will applaud and appreciate your growth

Fake **people** have an image to maintain. Real people just don't give a funk

Some **people** are going to leave, that's not the end of your story, that's the end of their part in your story.

I never listen to what **people** say, l just watch what they do. Behavior never lies.

I don't chase after **people** anymore if the like spending time with me they will do so. if not, l am content in my own company.

If you have to hurt other **people** in other to feel powerful, you are an extremely week individually

Pain changes **people,** some become rude and some become silent.

Shoutout to **people** whose kindness isn't a strategy but a way of life

Honestly having the right **people** around, you is the biggest life upgrade.

Some **people** are so focused on bringing others down that they fail to realize it's that mentality that keep them at the bottom

At your lowest you know the real faces of **people**

Accept **people** as they are, but place them where they belong.

Your lack of commitment is an insult to the **people** who believe in you.

Some **people** will be dancing in the flames of their pain and still send sparks out to light the way for others

People will forget what you said and people will forget what you did. But people will never forget how you made them feel.

Nobody realizes that some **people** expend tremendous energy merely to be normal.

Healing yourself can be offensive to **people** who benefited from your brokenness

When **people** tell you. you have changed, its only because you stopped acting, they way they want you to act.

Understand **people** by their actions and you will never be fooled by their words.

People go memories stay.

Every house has a smell that only the **people** living in the house don't smell.

At some point, **people's** intentions become irrelevant if their actions keep hurting you.

Sometimes it's not the **people** who changed; it's the mask that falls off.

Sometimes l wants to treat **people** how they treat me, but l don't because it's out of my character.

Honesty is a very expensive gift doesn't expect it from cheap **people.**

It's discouraging to think how **people** are shocked by honesty and how few by deceit.

Never being a good **person** just because of bad people.

People these days gain attention by losing respect.

The **people** who know the least about you always have the most to say .it's funny how that works

Quiet **people** have the loudest minds.

Some of the most generous people have no money. Some of the wisest **people** have no education. Some of the kindest **people** were hurt the most.

I'm aware that **people** talk behind my back. It's a pleasure to know that they don't have the guts to say it on my face.

People who get to bed and immediately fall asleep, don't you guys have problems.

Don't sacrifice your time for **people** who wouldn't do the same for you.

Some **people** never understand what you bring to the table until they watch you on action at another table.

I don't trust words anymore I trust actions. **People** can tell you anything but actions tell you everything

Damage **people** are strong because they know how to survive.

Some **people** will never support you because they are afraid of what you might become.

People cry not because they are weak, it's because they've been strong for too long.

People hurt you and then act like you hurt them.

If **people** don't like me, l don't care because l'm not born to entertain everyone,

Always stand up for yourself. **People** often step over those they think won't speak up for themselves.

Master the art of being finished with **people**. Not angry, not upset, just done.

People often come back in your life after they get disappointed by people, they thought were better than you.

Mouth can lie eye cannot. **People** will forget, Karma will not.

Fake **people** don't surprise me anymore loyal people do.

May be its true that **people** care when it's too late.

The only **people** who deserve to be in your life are those ones who treat you with love, kindness and respect,

People are not beautiful for the way the look, walk or talk. They are beautiful for the ways they love care and share.

I don't wish bad upon nobody but you reap what you sow in life. You don't treat **people** like shit and live a happy life.

I think l finally reach the point where l doesn't care anymore. **I'm a good person**; I can't force **people** to my worth.

The **person** you don't love is checking on you every day but the people you want in life are ignoring you every day.

When you build in silence **people** don't know what to attack.

I never lie, because l doesn't fear anyone **people** only lie when they are afraid.

Serve **people** what you can eat just in case plates are exchanged. This world is too small

I hope everyone loses their attachment to **people** who don't reciprocate their energy

You are just a visitor here. Do not try to become the owner of things and **people** because in reality nothing belongs to you.

Real situation exposes fake **people.**

The only **people**, I'm jealous of is the woman that stay home and their man pay all the bills ... You other ones NO.

Some **people** want material things Me; I just want peace, happy times, and people that love me.

People who do not understand your silence will never understand your words.

Life is too short to waste your time on **people** who don't respect, appreciate and value you.

Just be yourself. **People** don't have to like you. And you don't have to care.

Never forget the **people** who take time out of the day to check up on you.

There are **people** who will never stand by you because it's you, but there are those who will always back you because of who you are. You just need to find those who truly care about you.

If you knew how quickly **people** forget their sacked colleagues at work and the dead, you'd stop living to impress anybody

I leant that: You're not everyone's cup of tea the world is filled with **people**, who no matter what you do, no matter what you try, will simply not like you. But the world is also filled with those who will love you fiercely. The one who love you: They are Your **People**. Don't waste your finite time and heart trying to convince the people who aren't your people that you have value. They will miss it completely. They won't buy what you are selling. Don't try to convince them to walk your path with you because you will only waste your time and your emotional good health. You are not for them and they are not for you. You are not their cup of tea and they are not yours. Politely wave them along and you move away as well. Seek to share your path with those who recognize and appreciate your gifts, who you are. Be who you are. You are not everyone's cup of tea and that is OK.

So many **people** love you. Don't focus on the people who don't

Some **people** you thought loved you, only needed you.

There are very few **people** in your life who will openly tell you things you need to hear, rather than what you want to hear, no matter the consequences. Recognize those people early and always keep them close. They'll keep you going, they'll keep you sane, they'll humble you.

There will be **people** that would rather lose you, than be honest about what they've done to you. Let them go.

When you know who you are you don't need to waste time telling **people** who you are.

We live in a time where intelligent **people** are being silenced so that stupid people won't be offended.

Beautiful things happen when you distant yourself from stupid **people.**

Weak people revenge, Strong **people** forgive, intelligent people ignore.

Never judge **people** by their past. People learn, people change, people move on

Success is when you find **people** copying you.

You know, the world is full of lonely **people** afraid to make first move.

Be proof that good **people** with no hidden agendas still exist.

There is a time to be a nice **person** and there's a time to say enough is enough

I forgive **people** by forgetting them.

Your taste in **people** will change when you learn to love yourself

Pay attention to the way you feel around **people**. Energy never lies.

People who consistently and consciously hurt you do not deserve more chances. They deserve less access.

People will provoke you until the bring out the ugly side. Then play victim when you go there.

Be happy in front of **people** who don't like you, it kills them.

People still will lie directly to your face and then get mad at you because you don't trust them.

People who have overcome darkness in their life typically have a fire inside them that is almost impossible to extinguish.

Focus on **people** who love you. Not on people who don't

I hate those **people** who only talk to you when they need something.

I don't chase after **people** anymore, if they like spending time with me, they will do so. If not, I am content in my own company

Epilogue

What's in a book

A friend of ours was complaining to his doctor that he "couldn't understand **people**. Shaking his head, he added, I've read all sort of books on Psychology, studied mental hygiene, take a couple of year of "Psyche" in college. I can't understand it; people simply puzzle me "The doctor answered at once, "you're wasting your time reading books. You'll never understand people that way. You've got to live with people, work with them mix with them. Books aren't the whole story. I find them useful chiefly as guide to diagnose "Some people make the mistake of trying to learn about God merely by reading books about Him. To understand Him, you've got live with Him, work with Him, talk with Him, We do this in prayer, But we neglect to look for Him He is reflected in our fellowmen. "God is not far from anyone of us; for in Him we live and more and have our being. For we are His offspring. Act 17:28.

If you need to know people very well get out there and connect with people. "Quotes won't work unless you do it" Don't joke with this prayer: God connect me with people who matter to my purpose

Also by Fr. Mark Ngwah

You're Your Father's Daughter
You Need to Know People

About the Author

About the Author

Fr. Mark Ndifor OFM Cap is a dedicated Catholic priest belonging to the Franciscan Capuchin Friars. With a profound commitment to serving his community, Fr. Mark has spent over two decades in priesthood, embodying the values of compassion, empathy, and service.

Fr. Mark holds a **Master of Arts degree in Counseling Psychology**, earned through diligent study and dedication to understanding the complexities of the human psyche. His academic journey also includes a Bachelor of Arts in Counseling Studies from the University of Manchester, as well as a Higher Diploma in Counseling Studies. He is a registered member of the Kenya Association of Professional Counselors, showcasing his commitment to upholding the highest standards of professional practice in his field.

During his academic pursuits, Fr. Mark delved deep into the intricacies of father absence and its impact on daughters' self-esteem. His master dissertation, titled **"Influence of Absentee Fathers on Daughters' Self-Esteem in Selected Colleges in Ruiru Sub-County, Kiambu County, Kenya,"** sheds light on this crucial subject, offering valuable insights into the challenges faced by young women in the absence of paternal guidance.

As Fr. Mark celebrates his 25th year in priesthood, marking a remarkable silver jubilee in his service to God and community, he continues to be a beacon of hope and support for those in need. His unwavering dedication to helping others navigate the complexities of life has earned him respect and admiration from all who know him.

www.ingramcontent.com/pod-product-compliance
Lightning Source LLC
Chambersburg PA
CBHW051250160726
47994CB00003B/1105